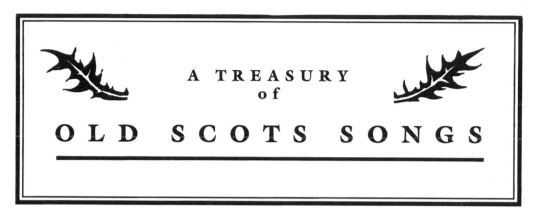

A TREASURY
of
OLD SCOTS SONGS

Edited and Arranged

by

G. Y. Cheyne & M. R. Cheyne

© Taigh na Teud 1995
Reprinted 1999

ISBN 1 871931 614

TAIGH NA TEUD
13 BREACAIS ARD
ISLE OF SKYE
SCOTLAND
IV42 8PY
email taighnateud@martin.abel.co.uk
www.abel.net.uk/~martin

For a catalogue of all Taigh na Teud publications, including the **"Ceol na Fidhle"**
and the **"Ceilidh Collection"** fiddle series, write to the publishers.

PREFACE

Folk-tunes are timeless, but every generation needs to interpret them afresh. This new collection aims at providing piano accompaniments which are straightforward, unpretentious, and above all tuneful; each arrangement is designed to lie within the technical grasp of amateur accompanists.

The tunes themselves have been selected solely on their musical merits, and no first-class Scottish air known to us has been excluded. Tunes for all vocal ranges are included. Some are clearly best interpreted by solo voice; others could well be sung by several voices in unison (as in schools).

The instrument closest to the human voice in its capacity to express emotion is the violin, and it is worth pointing out that all the tunes in this collection can be played on the violin in the first position. Every musician, whether aspiring beginner or experienced professional, will find in these old Scottish melodies a rare source of pleasure and interest.

The themes of the poems are as old as the human heart: love, war, and grief for untimely death predominate. The love may be love of the nation *(Scots, wha hae wi' Wallace bled)*, or love of a locality *(Whaur Gadie rins, Bonny Strathyre, The Isle of Mull)*, or even - hauntingly - the love of an immortal for a mortal *(Why should I sit and sigh?)*. But of course most of these poems celebrate love between the sexes; and here Scotland is supremely fortunate in possessing the greatest of all love poets, Robert Burns. Burns is now recognised not only as a poetic genius but as the foremost authority of his time on traditional Scottish songs. He had an infallible ear for a fine tune, and a unique ability to transform old words, or fashion new ones, to match a given melody. Half the songs in this collection come from his inspired pen.

G. Y. Cheyne and M. R. Cheyne
Peebles, 1995

CONTENTS

1. O gin I were a baron's heir

O gin I were a bar-on's heir, An' could I braid wi' gems your hair, And mak' ye braw as ye are fair, Lass-ie, would ye lo'e me? An' could I tak' ye tae the toun An' show ye braw sights mon-y a ain, And busk ye wi' a silk-en goun, Lass-ie, would ye lo'e me?

1. O gin I were a baron's heir,
An' could I braid wi' gems your hair,
And mak' ye braw as ye are fair,
Lassie, would ye lo'e me?
An' could I tak' ye tae the toun
An' show ye braw sights mony a ain,
And busk ye wi' a silken goun,
Lassie, would ye lo'e me?

2. Or should ye be content to prove,
In lowly life, unfading love,
A heart that nought on earth could move,
Lassie, would ye lo'e me?
And ere the lav'rock wing the sky,
Say, would ye to the forest hie,
And work wi' me sae merrily,
Lassie, would ye lo'e me?

3. And when the braw moon glistens o'er
Our lonesome bield an' heath'ry muir,
Will ye na greet that we're sae puir,
Lassie, for I lo'e ye?
For I ha'e nocht to offer ye,
Nae gowd frae mine, nae pearl frae sea,
Nor am I come o' high degree,
Lassie, but I lo'e ye!

Words traditional

2. Ho-ro, my nut-brown maiden

Moderato

ro, my nut - brown maid - en, Hi - ri, my nut - brown maid - en, Ho

ro___ ro___ maid - en, For she's the maid for me. Her___

eye so mild - ly beam - ing, Her___ look so fair and free, In___

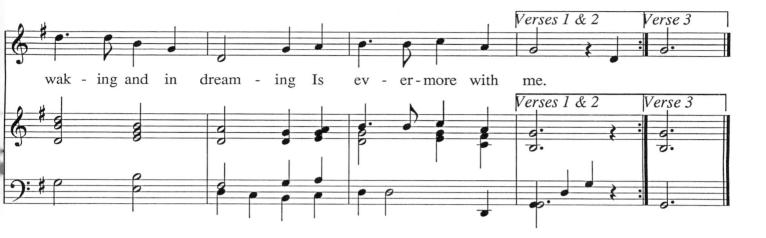

wak - ing and in dream - ing Is ev - er - more with me.

1. Ho-ro, my nut-brown maiden,
Hi-ri, my nut-brown maiden,
Ho ro ro, maiden,
For she's the maid for me.
Her eye so mildly beaming,
Her look so frank and free,
In waking and in dreaming
Is evermore with me.

2. O maiden, nut-brown maiden,
By land or on the sea,
Though time and tide may vary
My heart beats true for thee.
In Glasgow and Dunedin
Were maidens fair to see,
But ne'er a Lowland maiden
Could steal my love from thee.

3. And when with blossom laden
Bright summer comes again,
I'll fetch my nut-brown maiden
Down from her Highland glen.
Ho-ro, my nut-brown maiden,
Hi-ri, my nut-brown maiden,
Ho ro ro, maiden,
For she's the maid for me.

Original Gaelic author unknown.
Translation by J. S. BLACKIE

3. Ca' the yowes

8

3. Ca' the yowes

1. Ca' the yowes tae the knowes,
Ca' them whaur the heather grows,
Ca' them whaur the burnie rowes,
My bonny deary.
Hark, the mavis' evening sang
Sounding Clouden's woods amang;
Then a-faulding let us gang,
My bonny deary.

2. We'll gae down by Clouden side,
Through the hazels spreading wide
O'er the waves that sweetly glide
To the moon sae clearly.
Ghaist nor bogle shalt thou fear,
Thou'rt to Love and heav'n sae dear,
Nocht of ill may come thee near,
My bonny deary.

3. Fair and lovely as thou art,
Thou hast stol'n my very heart;
I can die - but canna part,
My bonny deary.
Ca' the yowes tae the knowes,
Ca' them whaur the heather grows,
Ca' them whaur the burnie rowes,
My bonny deary.

Words by BURNS

9

4. Whaur Gadie rins

O gin I were whaur Gad - ie rins, Whaur Gad - ie rins, Whaur Gad - ie rins, O gin I were whaur Gad - ie rins, At the back o' Benn - ach - ie. Aince mair to hear the wild birds' sang, To wan - der birks an' braes a - mang Wi' friends and fav' - rites

left sae lang At the back o' Benn - ach - ie. O gin I were whaur

Gad - ie rins, Whaur Gad - ie rins, Whaur Gad - ie rins, O gin I were whaur

Gad - ie rins At the back o' Benn - ach - ie.

1. O gin I were whaur Gadie rins,
Whaur Gadie rins, whaur Gadie rins,
O gin I were whaur Gadie rins
At the back o' Bennachie.
     Aince mair to hear the wild birds' sang,
     To wander birks an' braes amang
     Wi' friends and fav'rites left sae lang
     At the back o' Bennachie.
O gin I were whaur Gadie rins,
Whaur Gadie rins, whaur Gadie rins,
O gin I were whaur Gadie rins
At the back o' Bennachie.

2. How mony a day in blithe Springtime,
How mony a day in Summer's prime
I've saunterin' whiled awa the time
On the heights o' Bennachie.
     But fortune's flowers wi' thorns grow rife,
     An' wealth is won wi' toil an' strife;
     Gie me ae day o' youthfu' life
     At the back o' Bennachie.
O gin I were whaur Gadie rins,
Whaur Gadie rins, whaur Gadie rins,
O gin I were whaur Gadie rins
At the back o' Bennachie.

Words by J. PARK

5. The bonny Earl o' Moray

Ye Hie-lands and ye Low-lands, O whaur hae ye been? They hae slain the Earl o' Mor-ay, And laid him on the green. He was a braw gal-lant, And he rade at the ring, And the bon-ny Earl o' Mor-ay, He might have been a king. O lang will his la - dy look

frae the Cas-tle Doune Ere she see the Earl o' Mor-ay Come sound-in' through the toun.

1.Ye Hielands and ye Lowlands,
O, whaur hae ye been?
They hae slain the Earl o' Moray,
And laid him on the green.
He was a braw gallant,
And he rade at the ring,
And the bonny Earl o' Moray,
He might hae been a king.
    O lang will his lady
    Look frae the Castle Doune
    Ere she see the Earl o' Moray
    Come soundin' through the toun.

2. Now wae be to ye, Huntly,
And wherefore did ye sae?
I bade ye bring him wi' ye,
And forbade ye him to slay.
He was a braw gallant,
And he played at the glove;
And the bonny Earl o' Moray,
He was the Queen's true love.
    O lang will his lady
    Look frae the Castle Doune
    Ere she see the Earl o' Moray
    Come soundin' through the toun.

Author unknown

13

6. My love, she's but a lassie yet

Allegro giocoso

My love, she's but a lass - ie yet, My love, she's but a lass - ie yet; We'll let her stand a year or twa, She'll no be hauf sae sau - cy yet. My love, she's but a lass - ie yet, My love, she's but a lass - ie yet; We'll let her stand a year or twa, She'll no be hauf sae sau - cy yet. I rue the day I

legato

1. My love, she's but a lassie yet,
My love she's but a lassie yet;
We'll let her stand a year or twa,
She'll no be hauf sae saucy yet.
I rue the day I sought her O!
I rue the day I sought her O!
Wha gets her need na say he's woo'd,
But he may say he's bought her O!

2. Come draw a drap o' the best o't yet,
Come draw a drap o the best o't yet;
Gae seek for pleasure whar you will,
But here I never miss'd it yet.
We're a' dry wi' drinkin o't;
We're a' dry wi' drinkin o't;
The minister's kiss't the fiddler's wife;
He could na preach for thinkin o't.

3. My love, she's but a lassie yet,
My love she's but a lassie yet;
We'll let her stand a year or twa,
She'll no be hauf sae saucy yet.
I rue the day I sought her O!
I rue the day I sought her O!
Wha gets her need na say he's woo'd,
But he may say he's bought her O!

Words by BURNS

7. Sweet Afton

Flow gen - tly, sweet Af - ton, a - mang thy green braes! Flow gen - tly, I'll sing thee a song in thy praise; My Ma - ry's a - sleep by thy mur - mur - ing stream; Flow gen - tly, sweet Af - ton, dis - turb not her dream! Thou stock - dove, whose ech - o re -

16

1. Flow gently, sweet Afton, amang thy green braes!
Flow gently, I'll sing thee a song in thy praise;
My Mary's asleep by thy murmuring stream;
Flow gently, sweet Afton, disturb not her dream!
Thou stock-dove, whose echo resounds thro' the glen;
Ye wild whistling blackbirds, in yon thorny den!
Thou green crested lapwing, thy screaming forbear;
I charge you, disturb not my slumbering fair!

2. Thy crystal stream, Afton, how lovely it glides,
And winds by the cot where my Mary resides!
How wanton thy waters her snowy feet lave,
As gath'ring sweet flow'rets she stems thy clear wave!
Flow gently, sweet Afton, amang thy green braes!
Flow gently, sweet river, the theme of my lays!
My Mary's asleep by thy murmuring stream;
Flow gently, sweet Afton, disturb not her dream.

Words by BURNS

17

8. I'll ay ca' in by yon toun

I'll ay ca' in by yon toun And by yon gar-den green a-gain, I'll ay ca' in by yon toun To see my bon-ny Jean a-gain. There's nane shall ken and nane can guess What brings me back the gate a-gain But she, my fair-est faith-ful lass, And

1.   I'll ay ca' in by yon toun
       And by yon garden green again,
       I'll ay ca' in by yon toun
       To see my bonny Jean again.
There's nane shall ken and nane can guess
What brings me back the gate again
But she, my fairest faithful lass,
And secretly we'll meet again.
       I'll ay ca' in by yon toun
       And by yon garden green again,
       I'll ay ca' in by yon toun
       To see my bonny Jean again.

2.   I'll ay ca' in by yon toun
       And by yon garden green again,
       I'll ay ca' in by yon toun
       To see my bonny Jean again.
She'll wander by the oaken tree
When trysting time draws near again,
And when her lovely face I see
O faith! she's doubly dear again.
       I'll ay ca' in by yon toun
       And by yon garden green again,
       I'll ay ca' in by yon toun
       To see my bonny Jean again.

Words by BURNS

9. O can ye sew cushions?

O can ye sew cush - ions and can ye sew sheets? And can ye sing ba - lu - loo when the bairn greets? And hee and ba bird - ie, and hee and ba lamb! And hee and ba bird - ie, my bon - nie wee lamb!

1. O can ye sew cushions and can ye sew sheets?
And can ye sing baluloo when the bairn greets?
And hee and ba birdie, and hee and ba lamb!
And hee and ba birdie, my bonnie wee lamb!
    Hee O! wee O! what will I do wi' you?
    Black's the life that I lead wi' you!
    Mony o' you, little for to gi'e you,
    Hee O! wee O! what will I do wi' you?

2. I've placed my cradle on yon holly top;
And aye as the wind blew my cradle did rock.
O hush-a-ba baby, O ba lilly loo!
And hee and ba birdie, my bonnie wee doo!
    Hee O! wee O! what will I do wi' you?
    Black's the life that I lead wi' you!
    Mony o' you, little for to gi'e you,
    Hee O! wee O! what will I do wi' you?

Author unknown

21

10. O, I love the maiden fair

O, I love the maid-en fair, With her gold-en hair sae bon - ny, Dressed in silk - en gown sae rare, Thou hast left me drear - y.

Though I have but lit - tle gear I would strive to make thee mer - ry, Fish for sal - mon, chase the deer, All to please my dear - y.

1. O, I love the maiden fair,
With her golden hair sae bonny,
Dressed in silken gown sae rare,
Thou hast left me dreary.
Though I have but little gear,
I would strive to make thee merry,
Fish for salmon, chase the deer,
All to please my deary.

2. O, my heart is sad this day!
Shall it e'er again be cheery?
'Tis for thee my love I'm wae;
Would that I were near thee!
O, I love the maiden fair,
With her golden hair sae bonny,
Dressed in silken gown sae rare,
Thou hast left me dreary.

Original Gaelic author unknown.
Translation by H. WHYTE

11. Ae fond kiss

1. Ae fond kiss, and then we sever!
Ae fareweel, alas for ever!
Deep in heart-wrung tears I'll pledge thee,
Warring sighs and groans I'll wage thee.

Had we never lov'd sae kindly,
Had we never lov'd sae blindly,
Never met or never parted,
We had ne'er been broken hearted;
Broken hearted!

2. Fare thee weel, thou first and fairest!
Fare thee weel, thou best and dearest!
Thine be ilka joy and treasure,
Peace, enjoyment, love, and pleasure.

 Ae fond kiss, and then we sever!
Ae fareweel, alas for ever!
Deep in heart-wrung tears I'll pledge thee,
Warring sighs and groans I'll wage thee.
Ae fond kiss!

Words by BURNS

12. Leezie Lindsay

Will ye gang to the Hie - lands, Leez - ie Lind - say? Will ye gang to the Hie - lands wi' me? Will ye gang to the Hie - lands, Leez - ie Lind - say, My bride and my darl - ing to_____ be?

1. Will ye gang to the Hielands, Leezie Lindsay?
Will ye gang to the Hielands wi' me?
Will ye gang to the Hielands, Leezie lindsay,
My bride and my darling to be?

2."To gang to the Hielands wi' you, sir!
I dinna ken how that may be;
For I ken na the land that ye live in,
Nor ken I the lad I gang wi'."

3. He has led her high up on a mountain,
And bade her look out o'er the sea;
"These isles are Lord Ronald MacDonald's,
And his bride and his darling are ye!"

4. Then she kilted her coats o' green satin,
She has kilted them up to the knee,
And she's aff to the Hielands wi' Donald,
His bride and his darling to be.

Words by BURNS

13. The fair sailor lad

Andante con moto

O the fair sail-or lad He was hand-some and free, And he loved a gen-tle maid, And his wife she would be: "O my fair sail-or lad, Come and bide here wi' me!" But the fair sail-or lad sailed a-way, 'cross the sea.

D.C.

(Last time)

D.C. *p* *Rit.*

28

1. O the fair sailor lad
He was handsome and free,
And he loved a gentle maid,
And his wife she would be:
    "O my fair sailor lad,
    Come and bide here wi' me!" -
    But the fair sailor lad
    Sailed away, 'cross the sea.

2. O the fair sailor lad
He was wae and forlorn:
"I maun see yon gentle maid
From whose side I was torn."
    Tho' he sailed that very tide
    Her he saw not again,
    For that fair sailor lad
    Sleeps for aye 'neath the main.

3. O the fair sailor lad
He was handsome and free,
And he loved a gentle maid,
And his wife she would be:
    "O my fair sailor lad,
    Come and bide here wi' me!" -
    But the fair sailor lad
    Sleeps alone 'neath the sea.

Original Gaelic author unknown

14. Hey, Johnnie Cope

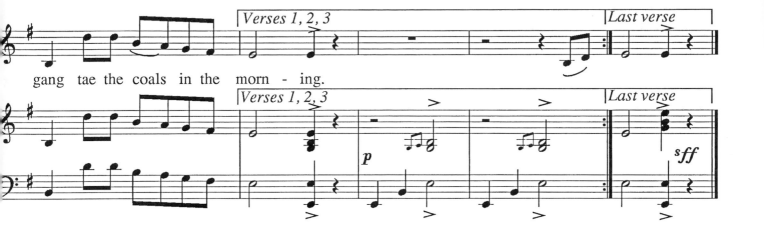

gang tae the coals in the morn - ing.

1. Cope sent a challenge frae Dunbar,
Saying, "Charlie, meet me an ye daur,
An I'll learn you the art o' war
If you'll meet me in the mornin'."

CHORUS:

  Hey , Johnnie Cope, are ye waukin yet?
  Or are your drums a-beatin yet?
  If ye are waukin I wad wait
  Tae gang tae the coals in the mornin'.

2.Now Johnnie, be as guid's your word,
Come let us try baith fire an sword,
An dinna flee like a frichtet bird
That's chased frae its nest in the mornin'.

  Hey, Johnnie Cope, &c.

3. Fie, Johnnie, noo get up and rin!
The Hieland bagpipes mak a din.
It's best to sleep in a hale skin,
For 'twill be a bludie mornin'.

  Hey, Johnnie Cope, &c.

4. When Johnnie Cope to Berwick came,
They spier'd at him, "Whaur's a' your men?" -
"The De'il confound me gin I ken,
For I left them a' in the mornin'."

  Hey, Johnnie Cope, &c

Words by A. SKIRVING

31

15. O lay thy loof in mine, lass

less thou'lt be my ain. O lay thy loof in mine, lass, in mine, lass, in mine, lass; And

swear on thy white hand, lass, that thou wilt be my ain.

1. O lay thy loof in mine, lass,
In mine, lass, in mine, lass;
And swear on thy white hand, lass,
That thou wilt be my ain.
     A slave to love's unbounded sway,
     He aft has wrought me meikle wae;
     But now he is my deadly fae,
     Unless thou'lt be my ain.
O lay thy loof in mine, lass,
In mine, lass, in mine, lass;
And swear on thy white hand, lass,
That thou wilt be my ain.

2. O lay thy loof in mine, lass,
In mine, lass, in mine, lass;
And swear on thy white hand, lass,
That thou wilt be my ain.
     There's mony a lass has broke my rest,
     That for a blink I hae lo'ed best;
     But thou art queen within my breast,
     Forever to remain.
O lay thy loof in mine, lass,
In mine, lass, in mine, lass;
And swear on thy white hand, lass,
That thou wilt be my ain.

Words by BURNS

16. O Willie's rare

1. O Willie's rare, and Willie's fair,
And Willie's wondrous bonnie;
And Willie hecht tae marry me
Gin e'er he married ony,
Gin e'er he married ony.

2. Yestreen I made my bed fu' braid,
The night I'll mak it narrow;
For a' the livelang winter night
I'll lie and dream o' Yarrow,
I'll lie and dream o' Yarrow.

3. O! cam ye by yon water side?
Pu'd ye a rose or lily?
Or cam ye by yon meadow green,
And saw ye my sweet Willie?
And saw ye my sweet Willie?

4. She sought him east, she sought him west,
She sought him braid and narrow;
Syne in the cliftin' o' a craig,
She found him drouned in Yarrow,
She found him drouned in Yarrow.

Author unknown

35

17. The gallant weaver

Where Cart rins row - in to the sea, By mon - y a flower and spread - ing tree, There lives a lad, the lad for me, He is a gall - ant Wea - ver. O I had woo - ers aught or nine, They gied me rings and rib - bons fine; And

I was fear'd my heart wad tine, And I gied it to the Wea - ver.

1. Where Cart rins rowin to the sea,
By mony a flower and spreading tree,
There lives a lad, the lad for me,
    He is a gallant Weaver.
O I had wooers aught or nine,
They gied me rings and ribbons fine;
And I was fear'd my heart wad tine,
And I gied it to the Weaver.

2. My daddie sign'd my tocher-band,
To gie the lad that has the land,
But to the heart I'll add my hand,
    And gie it to the Weaver.
While birds rejoice in leafy bowers,
While bees delight in opening flowers,
While corn grows green in summer showers,
I love my gallant Weaver.

Words by BURNS

18. The winter it is past

The win-ter it is past, and the sum-mer comes at last, And the small birds, they sing on ev'-ry tree; Now ev'-ry thing is glad, while I am ve-ry sad, since my true love is part-ed from me.

First 2 verses   Last verse

1. The winter it is past, and the summer comes at last,
    And the small birds, they sing on ev'ry tree;
Now ev'ry thing is glad, while I am very sad,
    Since my true love is parted from me.

2. The rose upon the brier, by the waters running clear,
    May have charms for the linnet or the bee;
Their little loves are blest, and their little hearts at rest,
    But my true love is parted from me.

3. My love is like the sun that in the sky doth run
    Forever so constant and true;
But his is like the moon that wanders up and doon,
    And ev'ry month it is new.

Words by BURNS

19. Ye banks and braes

Ye banks and braes o' bon - ny Doon, How can ye bloom sae fresh and fair? How can ye chant, ye lit - tle birds, And I sae wea - ry, fu' o' care! Thou'lt break my heart, thou warb - ling bird, That wan - tons thro' the flower - ing thorn: Thou minds me o' de - part - ed joys, De - part - ed nev - er to re - turn.

1. Ye banks and braes o' bonny Doon,
How can ye bloom sae fresh and fair?
How can ye chant, ye little birds,
And I sae weary, fu' o' care!
Thou'lt break my heart, thou warbling bird,
That wantons thro' the flowering thorn:
Thou minds me o' departed joys,
Departed never to return.

2. Aft hae I rov'd by bonny Doon,
To see the rose and woodbine twine;
And ilka bird sang o' its love,
And fondly sae did I o' mine;
Wi' lightsome heart I pu'd a rose,
Fu' sweet upon its thorny tree!
But my fause lover stole my rose,
And ah! he left the thorn wi' me.

Words by BURNS

20. Mary Morison

O Mar - y, at thy win - dow be, It is the wish'd, the tryst - ed hour! Those smiles and glan - ces let me see, That make the mis - er's trea - sure poor: How blythe - ly wad I bide the stour, A wear - y slave frae sun to sun, Could I the rich re - ward se - cure, the love - ly Mar - y Mor - i - son.

1. O Mary, at thy window be,
It is the wish'd , the trysted hour!
Those smiles and glances let me see,
That make the miser's treasure poor:
How blythely wad I bide the stour,
A weary slave frae sun to sun,
Could I the rich reward secure,
The lovely Mary Morison.

2. Yestreen, when to the trembling string
The dance gaed thro' the lighted ha',
To thee my fancy took its wing,
I sat, but neither heard nor saw:
Tho' this was fair , and that was braw,
And yon the toast of a' the town,
I sigh'd, and said among them a',
"Ye are na Mary Morison."

3. Oh, Mary, canst thou wreck his peace,
Wha for thy sake wad gladly die?
Or canst thou break that heart of his,
Whase only faut is loving thee?
If love for love thou wilt na gie
At least be pity to me shown;
A thought ungentle canna be
The thought o' Mary Morison.

Words by BURNS

21. A Hebridean love-lyric

Last night down by the sheil-ing Came Mai-ri, my be-lov-èd, Out on the hill-side, by the sheil-ing, My Mai-ri, my be-lov-èd O my fair one, O my rare one, O my Mai-ri, my be-lov-èd, There I sought her, there I found her, My Mai-ri, my be-lov-èd.

44

1. Last night down by the sheiling
    Came Mairi, my belovèd,
Out on the hillside, by the sheiling,
    My Mairi, my belovèd.
O my fair one, O my rare one,
    O my Mairi, my belovèd,
There I sought her, there I found her,
    My Mairi, my belovèd.

2. Like a lily on the waters
    Is Mairi, my belovèd,
A pure white lily on the waters
    Is Mairi, my belovèd.
None more lovely, none so gentle,
    None more lovely than my Mairi!
Let me fold thee in my bosom,
    My Mairi, my belovèd.

Gaelic author unknown

22. Why should I sit and sigh?

Why should I sit and sigh, pu' - ing brack - en, pu' - ing brack - en,

Why should I sit and sigh On the hill - side drear - y? When I see the

plov - er ris - ing, Or the cur - lew wheel - ing, Then I trow my mor - tal lov - er

Back to me is steal - ing. Why should I sit and sigh, Pu' - ing brack - en,

pu' - ing brack - en, Why should I sit and sigh All a - lone and wear - y?

1. Why should I sit and sigh,
     Pu'ing bracken, pu'ing bracken,
Why should I sit and sigh
     On the hillside dreary?
When I see the plover rising,
     Or the curlew wheeling,
Then I trow my mortal lover
     Back to me is stealing.
Why should I sit and sigh,
     Pu'ing bracken, pu'ing bracken,
Why should I sit and sigh
     All alone and weary?

2. When the day wears away,
     Sad I look a'down the valley;
Ilka sound wi' a stound
     Sets my heart a-thrilling.
Ah! but there is something wanting,
     Oh! but I am weary.
Come my blythe and bonnie lad,
     Come ower the knowe to cheer me.
Why should I sit and sigh,
     Pu'ing bracken, pu'ing bracken,
Why should I sit and sigh
     All alone and weary?

Words by JAMES HOGG

23. Fairy lullaby

I left my ba - by ly - ing here, A - ly - ing here, a - ly - ing here, I left my ba - by ly - ing here, And went to gath - er blae - ber - ries. Hò - van, hò - van, Gor - ry òg O, Gor - ry òg O, Gor - ry òg O, Hò - van, hò - van, Gor - ry òg O, I've lost my darl - ing ba - by, O!

1. I left my baby lying here,
A-lying here, a-lying here,
I left my baby lying here,
And went to gather blaeberries.

CHORUS:
Hòvan, hòvan, Gorry òg O,
Gorry òg O, Gorry òg O,
Hòvan, hòvan, Gorry òg O,
I've lost my darling baby, O!

2. I found the trace of dappled fawn,
Of dappled fawn, of dappled fawn,
I found the trace of dappled fawn,
But could not find my baby, O!

Hòvan, hòvan, &c.

3.I found the secret otter's track,
The otter's track, the otter's track,
I found the secret otter's track,
But could not find my baby, O!

Hòvan, hòvan, &c.

4. I found a trail of mountain mist,
Of mountain mist, of mountain mist,
I found a trail of mountain mist,
But could not find my baby, O!

Hòvan, hòvan, &c.

Original Gaelic author unknown

24. O whistle and I'll come to ye, my lad

Allegretto scherzando

O whist - le and I'll come to ye, my lad, O whist - le and I'll come to ye, my lad; Tho' faith - er and mith - er and a' should gae mad, O whist - le and I'll come to ye, my lad. But war - i - ly tent when ye come to court me, And come nae un - less the back - yett be a - jee; Syne up the back - style and let

nae-bod-y see, And come as ye were na com-in to me, O come as ye were na com-in to me.

rit.

1. O whistle and I'll come to ye, my lad,
 O whistle and I'll come to ye, my lad;
Tho' faither and mither an' a' should gae mad,
O whistle and I'll come to ye, my lad.
But warily tent when ye come to court me,
And come nae unless the back-yett be a-jee;
Syne up the back-style, and let naebody see,
And come as ye were na comin to me,
O come as ye were na comin to me.

2. O whistle and I'll come to ye, my lad,
 O whistle and I'll come to ye, my lad;
Tho' faither and mither an' a' should gae mad,
O whistle and I'll come to ye, my lad.
At kirk, or at market, whene'er ye meet me,
Gang by me as tho' that ye cared na' a flie;
But steal me a blink o' yer bonnie black e'e,
Yet look as ye were na lookin at me.
O look as ye were na lookin at me.

Words by BURNS

25. O my love is like a red, red rose

Andante appassionato

(Verse 3: *p*) O my

love is like a red, red rose That's new-ly sprung in June, O– my love is like a

mel-o-dy That's sweet-ly played in tune. As fair thou art, my bon-nie love, so

deep in love am I____; And I will love thee still, my dear, Till a' the seas gang dry.

1. O my love is like a red, red rose
    That's newly sprung in June,
O my love is like a melody
    That's sweetly played in tune.
As fair thou art, my bonnie love,
    So deep in love am I;
And I will love thee still, my dear,
    Till a' the seas gang dry.

2. Till a' the seas gang dry, my dear,
    And the rocks melt wi' the sun;
And I will love thee still, my dear,
    While the sands o' life shall run.
But fare thee weel, my only love,
    And fare thee weel a while;
And I will come again, my love,
    Tho' 'twere ten thousand mile.

3. O my love is like a red, red rose
    That's newly sprung in June,
O my love is like a melody
    That's sweetly played in tune.
But fare thee weel, my only love,
    And fare thee weel a while;
And I will come again, my love,
    Tho' 'twere ten thousand mile.

Words by BURNS

26. O this is no' my ain lassie

Allegretto

mf

O this is no' my ain lass-ie, Fair though the lass-ie be; O weel ken I my ain lass-ie, kind love is in her e'e.

Fine

I see a form, I see a face, Ye weel may wi' the

legato

fair-est place; It wants, to me, the witch-ing grace, The kind love that's in her e'e.

legato

CHORUS:

    O this is no' my ain lassie,
    Fair tho' the lassie be;
    O weel ken I my ain lassie,
    Kind love is in her e'e.

1. I see a form, I see a face,
Ye weel may wi' the fairest place;
It wants, to me, the witching grace,
The kind love that's in her e'e.

    O this is no my ain lassie, &c.

2. She's bonnie, blooming, straight, and tall,
And lang has had my heart in thrall;
And ay it charms my very saul,
The kind love that's in her e'e.

    O this is no my ain lassie, &c.

3. It may escape the courtly sparks,
It may escape the learned clerks,
But well the watching lover marks
The kind love that's in her e'e.

    O this is no my ain lassie, &c.

Words by BURNS

27. Bonny Strathyre

There's mead-ows in Lan-ark and mount-ains in Skye, And pas-tures in Hie-lands and Law-lands for-bye; But there's nae great-er luck that the heart could de-sire Than to herd the fine cat-tle in bon-ny Strath-yre. O it's up in the morn and a-wa to the hill, When the

56

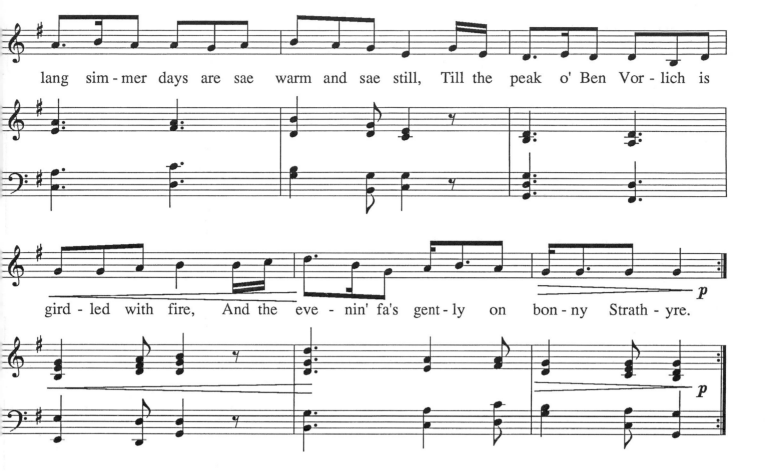

lang sim-mer days are sae warm and sae still, Till the peak o' Ben Vor-lich is

gird-led with fire, And the eve-nin' fa's gent-ly on bon-ny Strath-yre.

1. There's meadows in Lanark and mountains in Skye,
And pastures in Hielands and Lawlands forbye;
But there's nae greater luck that the heart could desire
Than to herd the fine cattle in bonny Strathyre.
O it's up in the morn and awa to the hill,
When the lang simmer days are sae warm and sae still,
Till the peak o' Ben Vorlich is girdled wi' fire,
And the evenin' fa's gently on bonny Strathyre.

2. Then there's mirth in the sheiling and love in my breast,
When the sun is gane doun and the kye are at rest;
For there's mony a prince wad be proud to aspire
To my winsome wee Maggie, the pride of Strathyre.
Her lips are like rowans in ripe simmer seen,
And mild as the starlicht the glint o' her e'en;
Far sweeter her breath than the scent of the briar,
And her voice is sweet music in bonny Strathyre.

3. Set Flora by Colin, and Maggie by me,
And we'll dance to the pipes swellin' loudly and free,
Till the moon in the heav'ns climbing higher and higher
Bids us sleep on fresh bracken in bonny Strathyre.
Though some to fine touns in the Lawlands will roam,
And some will gang sodgerin' far from their home;
Yet I'll aye herd my cattle, and bigg my ain byre,
And love my ain Maggie in bonny Strathyre.

Words by H. BOULTON

57

28. Over the sea to Skye

Speed, bon-nie boat, like a bird on the wing, On-ward! the sail-ors cry.

Car-ry the lad that's born to be king, O-ver the sea to Skye.

Loud the winds howl, loud the winds roar, Thun-der clouds rend the air.

1. Speed, bonnie boat, like a bird on the wing,
      Onward! the sailors cry.
Carry the lad that's born to be king,
      Over the sea to Skye.
Loud the winds howl, loud the winds roar,
      Thunderclouds rend the air.
Baffled, our foes stand by the shore;
      Follow they will not dare.
Speed, bonnie boat, like a bird on the wing,
      Onward! the sailors cry.
Carry the lad that's born to be king,
      Over the sea to Skye.

2. Sing me a song of a lad that is gone,
      Say, could that lad be I?
Merry of soul he sailed on a day
      Over the sea to Skye.
Mull was astern, Rum on the port,
      Eigg on the starboard bow;
Glory of youth glowed in his soul:
      Where is that glory now?
Speed, bonnie boat, like a bird on the wing,
      Onward! the sailors cry.
Carry the lad that's born to be king,
      Over the sea to Skye.

Words by H. BOULTON and R.L. STEVENSON

29. The lea-rig

Andante espressivo

p When o'er the hill the e'en - ing star Tells bught - in time is near, my jo, And ow - sen frae the fur - rowed field Re - turn sae dowf and wear - y O; Down by the burn, where birk - en buds Wi' dew are hang - in' clear, my jo, I'll

cresc.

meet thee on the lea_____ -rig My ain_____ kind_____ Dear - ie O.

1. When o'er the hill the e'ening star
    Tells bughtin time is near, my jo,
And owsen frae the furrow'd field
    Return sae dowf and weary O;
Down by the burn, where birken buds
    Wi' dew are hangin' clear, my jo,
I'll mcct thee on the lea-rig,
    My ain kind Dearie O.

2. At midnight hour, in mirkest glen,
    I'd rove, and ne'er be eerie O,
If thro' that glen I gaed to thee,
    My ain kind Dearie O;
Altho' the night were ne'er sae wild,
    And I were ne'er sae wearie O,
I'll meet thee on the lea-rig,
    My ain kind Dearie O.

3.The hunter lo'es the morning sun,
    To rouse the mountain deer, my jo;
At noon the fisher takes the glen
    Adown the burn to steer, my jo:
Gie me the hour o' gloamin grey,
    It maks my heart sae cheery O,
To meet thee on the lea-rig,
    My ain kind Dearie O.

Words by BURNS

30. A rose-bud by my early walk

rose - bud by my ear - ly walk, a - down a corn - in - clos - èd bawk, sae

gent - ly bent its thorn - y stalk, All on a dew - y morn - ing. Ere

twice the shades o' dawn are fled, In a' its crim - son glor - y spread, And

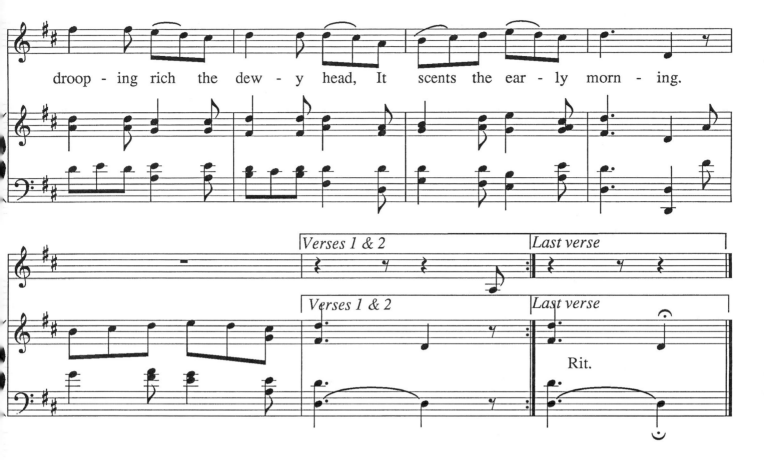

droop - ing rich the dew - y head, It scents the ear - ly morn - ing.

Verses 1 & 2   Last verse

1. A rose-bud by my early walk,
Adown a corn-inclosèd bawk,
Sae gently bent its thorny stalk,
      All on a dewy morning.
Ere twice the shades o' dawn are fled,
In a' its crimson glory spread,
And drooping rich the dewy head,
      It scents the early morning.

2. Within the bush her cover'd nest
A little linnet fondly prest;
The dew sat chilly on her breast,
      Sae early in the morning.
She soon shall see her tender brood,
The pride, the pleasure o' the wood,
Amang the fresh green leaves bedew'd,
      Awake the early morning.

3. So thou, dear bird, young Jeany fair,
On trembling string or vocal air,
Shall sweetly pay the tender care
      That tents thy early morning.
So thou, sweet Rose-bud, young and gay,
Shall beauteous blaze upon the day,
And bless the parent's evening ray
      That watch'd thy early morning.

Words by BURNS

63

31. Jock o' Hazeldean

Andante moderato

mf Why weep ye by the tide, la - dye? Why weep ye by the tide?____ I'll

wed ye to my young - est son, And ye shall be his bride; And

ye shall be his bride, la - dye, Sae come - ly to be seen - But

aye she loot the tears down fa' For Jock o' Haz - el - dean.

1. Why weep ye by the tide, ladye?
Why weep ye by the tide?
I'll wed ye to my youngest son,
And ye shall be his bride;
And ye shall be his bride, ladye,
Sae comely to be seen -
But aye she loot the tears down fa'
For Jock o' Hazeldean.

2. A chain o' gold ye shall not lack,
Nor braid to bind your hair,
Nor mettled hound, nor managed hawk,
Nor palfrey fresh and fair;
And you, the foremost o' them a',
Shall ride, our forest queen -
But aye she loot the tears down fa'
For Jock o' Hazeldean.

3. The kirk was deck'd at morning tide,
The taper glimmer'd fair,
The priest and bridegroom wait the bride,
And dame and knight are there.
They sought her baith by bower and ha',
The lady was not seen;
She's o'er the border, and awa'
Wi' Jock o' Hazeldean.

Words by Sir WALTER SCOTT

32. The Isle of Mull

Andante espressivo

The Isle of Mull is of isles the fair - est, Of oc - ean's gems 'tis the first and rar - est; green grass - y is - land of spark - ling foun - tains, of wav - ing woods and high tow' - ring moun - tains. Though far from home I am now a ran - ger, In grim New-

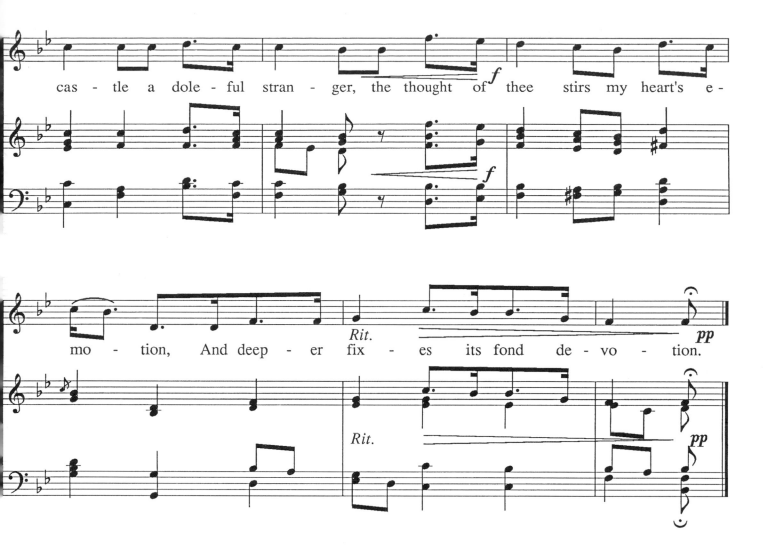

cas - tle a dole - ful stran - ger, the thought of *f* thee stirs my heart's e -

mo - tion, And deep - er fix - es its fond de - vo - tion.

1. The Isle of Mull is of isles the fairest,
Of ocean's gems 'tis the first and rarest;
Green grassy island of sparkling fountains,
Of waving woods and high tow'ring mountains.
Though far from home I am now a ranger,
In grim Newcastle a doleful stranger,
The thought of thee stirs my heart's emotion,
And deeper fixes its fond devotion.

2. How pleasant 'twas in the sweet May morning,
The rising sun thy bright fields adorning;
The larks above me their lays were singing,
While rocks and woods were with echoes ringing.
But gone are now all these joys forever,
Like bubbles bursting on yonder river;
Farewell, farewell to thy sparkling fountains,
Thy waving woods and high tow'ring mountains!

Gaelic original by D. MACPHAIL
Translation by M. MACFARLANE

33. Lord Ronald

Andante

O__ whaur hae ye__ been __, Lord Ron-ald, my__ son __? O__ whaur__ hae ye been__, Lord Ron-ald __, my__ son? I hae been wi' my__ sweet-heart, mo-ther, mak my bed soon __, For I'm wear-y wi' the hunt-ing, and fain wad__ lie__ doon.

Verse 1 | *Last vers*

1. O whaur hae ye been, Lord Ronald, my son?
O whaur hae ye been, Lord Ronald, my son?
I hae been wi' my sweetheart, mother, mak my bed soon,
For I'm weary wi' the hunting, and fain wad lie doon.

2. What got ye frae your sweetheart, Lord Ronald, my son?
What got ye frae your sweetheart, Lord Ronald, my son'?
I hae got a deadly poison, mother, mak my bed soon,
For life is a burden that soon I'll lay doon.

Author unknown

34. The lass of Patie's mill

The lass of Pat - ie's mill____, So bon - nie, blythe, and gay, In____ spite of all my skill____, She stole my heart a - way. When ted - ding of the hay____, Bare - head - ed on the green, Love 'midst her locks did play, And wan - ton'd in her een.

Verses 1&2 | Last verse

1. The lass of Patie's mill,
So bonnie, blythe, and gay,
In spite of all my skill
She stole my heart away.
When tedding of the hay,
Bare-headed on the green,
Love 'midst her locks did play,
And wanton'd in her e'en.

2. Without the help of art,
Like flow'rs which grace the wild,
She did her sweets impart,
Whene'er she spoke or smiled.
Her looks they were so mild,
Free from affected pride,
She me to love beguiled;
I wish'd her for my bride.

3. O! had I all the wealth
Hopetoun's high mountains fill;
Insured long life and health,
And pleasure at my will;
I'd promise and fulfil
That none but bonnie she,
The lass of Patie's mill,
Should share the same with me.

Words by ALLAN RAMSAY

35. The flowers o' the forest

Adagio espressivo

I've heard them lilt___ in'___ at the ewe milk - in',

Lass - es a - lilt - in' be - fore___ dawn of day. Now there's a moan - in' on

il - ka green___ loan - in', The Flowers o' the For - est are a' wede a - way.

ten. *rit.*

Verses 1, 2 & 3   Last verse

Verses 1, 2 & 3   Last verse

a tempo   *morendo*

1. I've heard them liltin' at the ewe milkin',
Lasses a-liltin' before dawn of day.
Now there's a moanin' on ilka green loanin',
The Flowers o' the Forest are a' wede away.

2.At bughts in the mornin', nae blithe lads are scornin',
Lasses are lanely, and dowie, and wae;
Nae daffin, nae gabbin, but sighin' and sabbin',
Ilk ane lifts her leglin, and hies her away.

3. At e'en in the gloamin', nae swankies are roamin'
'Bout stacks wi' the lasses at bogle to play;
But ilk maid sits drearie, lamentin' her dearie,
The Flowers o' the Forest are a' wede away.

4. We'll hae nae mair liltin' at the ewe milkin',
Women and bairns are heartless and wae;
Sighin' and moanin' on ilka green loanin',
The Flowers o' the Forest are a' wede away.

Words by JANE ELLIOT

36. Scots, wha hae wi' Wallace bled

Scots, wha hae wi' Wal - lace bled! Scots, wham Bruce has af - ten led__,

Wel - come to your go - ry bed, Or to vic - to - rie!

Now's the day, and now's the hour: See the front of bat - tle lour:

See ap-proach proud Ed-ward's power - Chains and sla-ver-ie!

Verses 1 & 2 | Last verse

1. Scots, wha hae wi' Wallace bled!
Scots, wham Bruce has aften led,
Welcome to your gory bed,
    Or to victorie!
Now's the day and now's the hour:
See the front of battle lour:
See approach proud Edward's power -
    Chains and slaverie!

2. Wha will be a traitor knave?
Wha can fill a coward's grave?
Wha sae base as be a slave?
    Let him turn and flee!
Wha, for Scotland's king and law,
Freedom's sword will strongly draw,
Freeman stand, or freeman fa',
    Let him on wi' me!

3. By oppression's woes and pains!
By your sons in servile chains!
We will drain our dearest veins,
    But they shall be free!
Lay the proud usurper low!
Tyrants fall in every foe!
Liberty's in every blow! -
Let us do - or die!

Words by BURNS

37. Ay waukin', O!

Wauk - in' ay, an' ee - rie, Sleep I can - na get, For think - in' on my dear - ie;

Ay wauk - in', O! *pp*

Rit.

Coda

pp

CHORUS:
  Ay waukin', O!
  Waukin' ay, an' eerie;
  Sleep I canna get,
  For thinkin' on my dearie;
  Ay waukin', O!

1. Spring's a pleasant time,
Flow'rs of ev'ry colour;
The water rins o'er the heugh,
And I long for my lover.

    Ay waukin', O! &c.

2. When I sleep I dream,
When I wauk I'm eerie;
Rest I can get nane,
For thinkin' on my dearie.

    Ay waukin', O! &c.

3. Lanely night comes on,
A' the lave are sleepin';
Think on my bonnie lad,
An' blear my e'en wi' greetin'.

    Ay waukin', O! &c.

Words by BURNS

Glossary

Note:- The English equivalent of a Scottish word can often be deduced by altering the vowel sound (e.g., goun=gown, sae =so, tae=to, wad=would) or by adding a consonant (e.g., gi'e=give, no'=not, wi'=with). There is no consistency in the spelling of Scottish words, partly because of regional differences in pronunciation.

ae=one
a-fauldin=folding cattle at nightfall
aff=off
aft=often
ain=own
a-jee=ajar
an ye daur=if you dare
are ye waukin yet?=are you awake yet?
aught=eight
awa=away
ay=always
aye=ever

back-style=back stair
back-yett=back gate
baith=both
bawk=a narrow path
bide=abide
bide the stour=endure the struggle
bield=shelter
bigg=build
birk=birch tree
birken buds=birch buds
blaeberry=bilberry
blear=blur, inflame
blink=(1)short space of time (2)glance
bludie=bloody
bogle=ugly phantom
brae=slope of small hill
braid=broad
braw=elegant, fine, splendid
bught=sheepfold
bughtin time=time for folding sheep at nightfall
burnie=streamlet
busk=adorn, dress splendidly
byre=cowshed, farm building

ca'=call
cliftin'=fissure, cleft
craig=rock

daffin=merrymaking
daur=dare
dinna=do not
doon=down
dowf=dispirited
dowie=melancholy

een=eyes
eerie=melancholy

fae=foe
fain=willingly
faulding=folding of sheep at nightfall
frae=from
frichtet=frightened

gabbin=gossiping
gae=go
gang=go
gang tae the coals=go to work(?)
ghaist=ghost
gi'e=give
gin=if
gin I were=would that I were
gloamin=twilight
goun=gown
gowd=gold
greet=weep
guid=good

hae=have

hale=undamaged

hauf=half

hecht=vowed

heugh=crag

hielands=highlands

I dinna ken=I don't know

ilk, ilka=every

jo=sweetheart

ken=know

kilt (verb)=tuck up clothing

knowe=knoll

kye=cattle

lanely=lonely

lang=long

lave=rest, others

lav'rock=skylark

lea-rig=ridge of unploughed grass

Leezie=Lizzie (diminutive of Elizabeth)

leglin=milking-pail

lilting=singing sweetly without words

loaning=grassy farm-track

lo'e=love

loof=palm of hand

loot=let

maun=must

mavis=song-thrush

meikle=much

mony=many

na=not

nae=no

nane=none

nocht=nothing

ony=any

owsen=oxen

played at the glove=took part in sport of hawking

rade at the ring=rode in tournaments

rowe=roll

rowin=rolling

sabbin=sobbing

sae=so

sang=song

sheiling=remote summer pasture

sodgering=soldiering

speir'd at=questioned

stound=pang

stour=struggle

swankie=strapping young man

syne= at last

tae=to

tedding=spreading out to dry

tent=mark, take heed

tine=suffer loss, cease to enjoy

tocher-band=marriage agreement

toun=(1)town, (2)a farm estate

trow=believe

wad=would

wae (noun)=woe

wae (adjective)=wretchedly sad

waukin=awake

wede away=carried off by death

weel=well

wha=who

wham=whom

whar, whaur=where

wi=with

yestreen=last night

yon=that

yowes=ewes

Notes

Song 1 (O gin I were a baron's heir).

Joseph William Holder (1765-1832), the composer of this tune, was in fact English by birth. A graduate in Music of Oxford University, he has here produced what the Editor of *Scots Minstrelsie* (1893) called "a very pleasing imitation of the Scotch style."

Song 2 (Ho-ro, my nut-brown maiden).

John Stuart Blackie (1809-1895) who translated the Gaelic words of this old Highland air, was Professor of Humanity (i.e., Latin) at the University of Aberdeen and subsequently Professor of Greek at Edinburgh University. Among his many interests were the teaching of Gaelic and the translation of traditional Gaelic songs. In Greig's *Scots Minstrelsie* (1892-1895) the Gaelic poet is named as "Mr. Sinclair", but no other details are given.

Song 3 (Ca' the yowes).

Burns heard this tune sung to traditional words by a Markinch schoolmaster, the Rev. John Clunie, and immediately recognised its merits. Retaining the opening four lines of the old poem, he added new words for the version given here. It was first published in Johnson's *The Scots Musical Museum* of 1790. Burns sets the scene of his verses on the banks of the river Clouden, a tributary of the Nith, not far from his farm at Ellisland, north of Dumfries.

Song 4 (Whaur Gadie rins).

The Gadie, an insignificant tributary of the river Don in Aberdeenshire, has probably inspired more adulatory verse than any stream of comparable size in the world. It runs "at the back of" - i.e., to the north of - Bennachie, a finely-shaped hill which dominates the landscape of eastern Aberdeenshire. Because of the exceptional charm of their surroundings, and perhaps also because of this poem, Bennachie and the Gadie burn continue to draw visitors from far and wide.

Dr. John Park (1805-1865) was a Presbyterian minister at St. Andrews when he wrote these verses, which it is said he took down from the singing of a "peasant girl" in the Aberdeenshire Highlands.

The tune is the air *The Hessians' March.*

Song 5 (The bonny Earl o' Moray).

This poem recalls a lurid period of Scottish history, when high passion, jealousy, and intrigue were rife among members of the nobility, with murder a frequent consequence.

The youthful earl of Moray had many enemies in high places: there was a long-standing land-feud with the Earl of Huntly, and another with the Earl of Argyll and the Campbells. The king, James VI, had a private reason for hating him, having apparently overheard the Queen praising Moray as "a proper and gallant man" - epithets no-one could ever have applied to James. In 1592 James was prevailed upon to issue a warrant for Moray's arrest, but Huntly was in no mood for half-measures: Moray was brutally struck down by several assassins, including Huntly, outside his castle in Fife. The Earl's corpse was taken by his mother, Lady Doune, to Holyrood Palace, where the King chose to ignore it. It lay for months uninterred. No action was taken by the King against the assassins.

The words of the poem, which is very old, are enigmatic. Due regard is given to the Earl's well documented physical beauty, to his prowess in falconry and jousting, and it is even boldly declared that "he was the Queen's true love", and that "he might have been a king". But who is supposed to be the speaker? "I bade ye bring him wi' ye, and forbade ye him to slay" - it can only be the King himself uttering those words! Perhaps the writer of the poem guessed that the King, though conniving at the murder, might be haunted by memories of his peerless courtier, and would need to give utterance to a conscience-stricken grief.

Song 6 (My love, she's but a lassie yet).

This tune was first printed in 1757 as *Miss Farquharson's Reel*, but under another title, *My love she's but a lassie yet,* in 1782. Burns adopted the latter title as the basis of his song, which was published in *The Scots Musical Museum* of 1790.

Song 7 (Sweet Afton).

The Afton is a tributary of the Nith, the river near Burns's farm at Ellisland, Dumfries. The "Mary" of this poem may be Mary Campbell, so-called "Highland Mary" - one of Burns's many paramours - or simply a creature of the poet's imagination.

Alexander Hume (1811-1859) who composed the tune given here was an accomplished musician, but this is the only work by which he is now remembered.

Song 8 (I'll aye ca' in by yon toun).

Burns took the old ballad *I'll gang nae mair to yon town* and whimsically reversed the intention there expressed. His future wife Jean Armour is the "Bonny Jean" referred to in the poem.

The tune is that of the original ballad. It was first printed in *Bremner's Scots Reels* of 1757.

Song 9 (O can ye sew cushions).

Johnson's *The Scots Musical Museum* of 1796 contains this beautiful cradle-song, but nothing is known of either the writer of the verses or the composer of the melody.

Song 10 (O, I love the maiden fair).

From Moffat's *Minstrelsy of the Scottish Highlands* (1907). Henry Whyte, the translator of the Gaelic words, was an active collector of Gaelic folk-tunes towards the end of the 19th century. Many well-known Gaelic songs survived because of his efforts.

Song 11 (Ae fond kiss).

Burns met and fell in love with Mrs. Nancy McLehose in Edinburgh in 1787. She was beautiful and witty; he was the young literary lion of his day. They conducted a famous correspondence ("Sylvander" to "Clarinda") but parted forever on 6 December 1791. Burns sent her these verses soon after. Sir Walter Scott said of them that they "contain the essence of a thousand love tales".

The tune given here is an old melody published in *Greig's Scots Minstrelsie* of 1892-1895.

Song 12 (Leezie Lindsay).

Burns "collected" the tune, and included the first four lines of the original ballad in his new version. The complete poem was first published in Jamieson's *Popular Ballads* of 1806.

Song 13 (The fair sailor lad).

From Moffat's *Minstrelsy of the Scottish Highlands* (1907), where the Gaelic words of Hebridean origin are translated by Henry Whyte (see note to Song 10).

Song 14 (Hey, Johnnie Cope).

The battle of Prestonpans (21 September 1745) was fought between the rebel Highland army of Prince Charles Edward Stewart - "Bonny Prince Charlie", the "Young Pretender" to the British throne - and the Government forces of King George II under Sir John Cope. Cope's well-armed and highly trained battalions disintegrated before a furious assault by the Highlanders, whereupon Cope himself fled with great speed to Berwick, becoming (in the words of a sarcastic onlooker) "the first General in Europe who had brought the first tidings of his own defeat."

Adam Skirving's ironic, blood-thirsty verses portray the whole affair very much from the victorious Jacobite view-point. Skirving, a farmer from Haddington, was an able versifier, and reportedly "one of the wittiest and most whimsical of mankind".

This tune was first published in *The Scots Musical Museum* of 1790.

Song 15 (O lay thy loof in mine, lass).

This love-poem remained unpublished until seven years after the poet's death. The subject was probably Jessie Lewars, the sister of Burns's friend John Lewars. Ironically, it was Jessie Lewars who was to nurse Burns during his brief fatal illness.

The melody, *The Cordwainer's March*, was published in Aird's *Airs* of 1782.

Song 16 (O Willie's rare).

The words appear in Allan Ramsay's *Tea-table Miscellany* of 1724, and the complete song, with its traditional air, in Johnson's *The Scots Musical Museum* of 1803.

Song 17 (The gallant weaver)

An authority on the songs of Burns claims that this tune lacks the character of a Scottish melody, resembling *The New Swedish Dance* published in 1715. Swedish or Scottish, the tune as it stands certainly suits Burns's words admirably, with the repetitive click-clack of a weaver's shuttle audible in its rhythms.

Paisley, the centre of the Scottish weaving industry, grew up on the banks of the river Cart, where Burns's "gallant weaver" was supposed to live.

Song 18 (The winter it is past).

Burns based his poem on the words of *The Lovesick Maid*, a popular ballad about a highwayman hanged in 1750. By excising references to that incident, and concentrating on the grief all lovers feel on parting, whether temporarily or permanently, Burns succeeded in strengthening the earlier poem immeasurably.

The melody was first published in the *Caledonian Pocket Companion* of 1759.

Song 19 (Ye banks and braes)

Three versions by Burns of this famous poem about a deserted lover are known, of which this is the last and best. The Doon river winds through a romantic glen on its way from Loch Doon to the sea near Ayr.

The tune, *The Caledonian Hunt's Delight,* was (according to Burns) written by a Mr. James Miller with the assistance of Burns's friend Stephen Clarke, the Edinburgh musician who undertook the harmonisation of the tunes in Johnson's *The Scots Musical Museum,* to which Burns contributed many songs. A tradition persists, however, that the tune is of Irish origin. It was first published by the eminent Scots fiddler Neil Gow in his *Second Collection of Strathspey Reels* of 1788.

The final version of the song was published in Johnson's *The Scots Musical Museum* of 1792.

Song 20 (Mary Morison).

Much ink has been spilt trying to identify the subject of this poem, yet it is quite likely that Burns merely chose a name which suited the rhythms of the melody. It is an early work, dismissed by the poet himself as "juvenile"; on publication, however, its popularity was immediate.

The tune, *Duncan Davison*, was published in McGlashan's *Strathspey Reels* of 1780.

Song 21 (A Hebridean love-lyric).

In the early years of this century Marjorie Kennedy-Fraser, a talented musician and composer, visited the Outer Hebridean Islands in search of traditional songs. This fine example was sung to her by Ann Macneill, an inhabitant of Barra, an island noted for its native melodies. Gaelic verses (freely translated here) were added by Kenneth Macleod, a native of the islands and an authority on Hebridean culture.

Song 22 (Why should I sit and sigh?).

James Hogg, the "Ettrick Shepherd", was a contemporary and friend of Sir Walter Scott, and like Scott he wrote both novels and poems with a strong Scottish flavour. Often, as in this curious poem, his work has eerie supernatural overtones.

Song 23 (Fairy lullaby).

This haunting song about an infant stolen by fairies appears in Moffat's *Minstrelsy of the Scottish Highlands* (1907), with a translation by Lachlan MacBean, who edited *The Scottish Songs and Hymns of the Gael.*

Song 24 (O whistle and I'll come to ye, my lad).

Burns himself identified Jean Lorimer as the heroine of these verses. The tune, and the first four lines, are traditional. An early version of Burns's poem was published in *The Scots Musical Museum* of 1788, and the revised song was printed in the *Select Collection of Original Scotish* (sic) *Airs* of 1799.

Song 25 (O my love is like a red, red rose).

Burns's most famous song, seeming to embody all the qualities for which as a song-writer he is renowned. Yet his actual authorship of the poem is disputed, not least because of his reported admission that he copied the words from a country girl's singing. What seems likely is that the poet revised and transformed those original words, adding such touches of genius as resulted in the song becoming one of his masterpieces.

The tune, *Major Graham*, appeared first in Gow's *Strathspeys* of 1784.

Song 26 (O this is no' my ain lassie).

This tune, with the title *This is no my ain house* was printed in *Orpheus Caledonius* of 1733; but verses by the poet Allan Ramsay with the same title had appeared (without music) in Ramsay's *Tea-table Miscellany*. Burns recast Ramsay's poem, altering it almost out of recognition, but retaining the rhythms of the old tune.

It was published in Thomson's *Select Collection of Original Scotish* (sic) *Airs* of 1799.

Song 27 (Bonny Strathyre).

A pleasing concoction from the pen of Sir Harold Boulton, a Victorian composer, versifier, and musicologist. In *Songs of the North*, edited by MacLeod and Boulton (1855), it is stated that the tune is adapted from an old air *Taymouth*. Those familiar with the jig *The muckin' o' Geordie's byre* will detect a strong similarity. Boulton may have, as it were, found the tune in the cowshed, but having subjected it to a little judicious laundering he was able quite happily to introduce it into the Victorian drawingroom.

Song 28 (Over the sea to Skye).

The "lad that's born to be king" was Prince Charles Edward Louis Philip Casimir, the "Young Pretender" who led the last Jacobite attempt to reinstate the Stewarts on the British throne. A grandson of King James VII, he was under 25 years of age when he raised the Royal Standard at Glenfinnan on 19 August 1745. Sweeping through Scotland, gathering support all the way, he routed Sir John Cope's forces at Prestonpans (see song 14), crossed the Border to seize Carlisle, and reached as far south as Derby by December 4. There his luck, and many of his supporters, began to desert him. A long retreat northwards followed, and the remnant of his Highland army suffered a decisive defeat at Drummossie Moor, near Culloden, outside Inverness, on 16 April 1746. Thereafter the Prince, with a price of £30,000 on his head, wandered through the Highlands and Islands as a fugitive, relying on the loyalty of individuals like the brave Flora Macdonald to save him from arrest. He sailed for France on 20 September 1746; with his departure the Jacobite adventure was finally at an end.

The words of the first stanza of the song (a Victorian *pastiche*) refer to the period when the Prince was fleeing from his pursuers, but Stevenson's haunting lines in the second stanza recall the bright days at the start of the campaign, when the handsome young Chevalier, confident of his powers, still believed it was his destiny to wear a crown.

The melody is also Victorian, though it possibly had its origin in a Gaelic folk-tune. Its rhythms suggest the beat of oars, and Gaelic oarsmen often sang to such rhythms while plying their craft between the islands of the Hebrides.

Song 29 (The lea-rig).

Burns has here remoulded and extended a poem of the same name by the Edinburgh poet Robert Fergusson (1750-74). The tune, *My ain kind dearie, O*, was published, but not with Burns's words, in *The Scots Musical Museum*.

Song 30 (A rosebud by my early walk).

The "Jeany" of this poem was Jeany Cruikshank, the 12-year-old daughter of Burns's friend William Cruikshank, in whose house Burns lodged from September 1787 to February 1788. Jeany played the harpsichord well, and Burns got her to play over on that instrument the melodies for which he was then writing words. In return, he wrote for her this beautiful poem.

The tune given here is a traditional melody, *The Shepherd's Wife*.

Song 31 (Jock o' Hazeldean).

The first stanza of this ballad is said to be ancient. Scott wrote the others for Campbell's *Albyn Anthology* of 1816.

The melody is based on an old tune *Willie and Annet*.

Song 32 (The Isle of Mull).

From Moffat's *The Minstrelsy of the Scottish Highlands* (1907). Dugald McPhail (1818-87), a native of Torosay on the island of Mull, is said to have written these words while working in the busy industrial town of Newcastle in the north of England. Nothing is known concerning the origin of the beautiful melody.

Song 33 (Lord Ronald).

This ancient ballad was "collected" by Burns in Ayrshire and sent by him, along with its traditional melody, to *The Scots Musical Museum* of 1792. Sir Walter Scott, in his *Minstrelsy of the Scottish Border* gives a very similar but longer ballad, entitled *Lord Randal*. Scott suggests that the original subject of the ballad was Thomas Randolph, or Randal, Earl of Murray and nephew of King Robert Bruce: "This great warrior died at Musselburgh in 1332, at the moment when his services were most necessary to his country, already threatened by an English army. For this sole reason, perhaps, our historians obstinately impute his death to poison."

Song 34 (The lass o' Patie's mill).

Patie's mill stood on the banks of the river Irvine, which flows into the sea north of Ayr. The poet Allan Ramsay, walking near the mill with his friend the Earl of Loudoun, had his attention drawn to "a rustic girl of uncommon beauty" spreading hay in a nearby field. His lordship observed that the girl would make a fine subject for a song; and within hours the poem was completed.

The melody, which is very old, was published in *Orpheus Caledonius* of 1725. In his *Caledonian Companion* of 1743 James Oswald, on dangerously slender evidence, identifies the composer as the Italian David Rizzio, Mary Queen of Scots' secretary, music-master, *valet de chambre*, and perhaps lover, who was brutally done to death in Holyrood Palace in 1566 (his bloodstains are still shown to visitors by helpful guides).

Whether or not the attribution to Rizzio is correct, one must admit that there is about this tune a curiously Italian flavour which is hard to explain.

Song 35 (The Flowers of the Forest).

At Flodden, 12 miles south of Berwick-upon-Tweed, on 9 September 1513, an invading Scottish army suffered overwhelming defeat at the hands of an English army under the Earl of Surrey. The Scottish King James IV and some 10,000 of his subjects perished, among them the leaders of nearly all the great Scottish families, as well as the "Flowers of the Forest" - the young men, renowned for their beauty and strength, from the region of southern Scotland anciently known as the Forest of Jed.

The first line of Jane (or Jean) Elliot's poem of 1756 is from a traditional lament for the Flodden dead. No other work by her survives. She was a daughter of Sir Gilbert Elliot of Minto, and lived from 1727 to 1805. Legend has it that she was the last woman in Edinburgh to make regular use of her own sedan-chair.

The melody first appears in the Skene manuscript of music for treble lute (early 17th century).

Song 36 (Scots wha hae wi' Wallace bled).

At Bannockburn near Stirling, on 24 June 1314, a force of 30,000 Scots under King Robert Bruce routed a much larger combined English, Welsh and Irish army. The English king, Edward II, fled the field, leaving behind him what Sir Walter Scott probably correctly described as "the finest army a king of England ever commanded." Bruce went on to secure complete independence for Scotland.

Burns's friend John Syme relates how one day in August 1793 he and the poet were riding across a desolate Scottish moor: "The hollow wind sighed; the lightnings gleamed; the thunder rolled. The poet enjoyed the awful scene - he spoke not a word, but seemed wrapt in meditation. What do you think he was about? He was charging the English army along with Bruce at Bannockburn."

The next day Burns completed the poem, which purports to be Bruce's Address to his Troops before Battle. Burns himself chose the melody given here, stating that there was a widely-held tradition in Scotland that it was to this tune, "Hey tuttie taitie", that Bruce's conquering army had marched towards Bannockburn. The song, with Burns's words and this tune, appeared in *The Scots Musical Museum* of 1803.

Song 37 (Ay waukin', O!)

From Johnson's *Scots Musical Museum* of 1790. Burns based his poem on a traditional lyric, which he altered considerably. In this simple but poignant song he seems to have achieved that ultimate aim of song-writers - a perfect blend of words and melody.

TITLE	KEY	RANGE
1. O gin I were a baron's heir	F	C-D
2. Ho-ro, my nut-brown maiden	G	D-E
3. Ca' the yowes	Am	C-E
4. Whaur Gadie rins	A	A-E
5. The bonny Earl o' Moray	B♭	D-D
6. My love, she's but a lassie yet	A	A-F♯
7. Sweet Afton	G	B-D
8. I'll aye ca' in by yon toun	E	E-E
9. O can ye sew cushions?	D	A-D
10. O, I love the maiden fair	A	C♯-F♯
11. Ae fond kiss	D	D-E
12. Leezie Lindsay	F	C-F
13. The fair sailor lad	A	E-E
14. Hey, Johnnie Cope	Em	B-E
15. O lay thy loof in mine, lass	Am	E-F
16. O Willie's rare	G	A-E
17. The gallant weaver	B♭	D-E♭
18. The winter it is past	F	F-F
19. Ye banks and braes	G	D-E
20. Mary Morison	Dm	D-F
21. A Hebridean love-lyric	G	B-E
22. Why should I sit and sigh?	Em	D-E
23. Fairy lullaby	G	D-D
24. O whistle and I'll come to ye, my lad	B♭	C-G
25. O my love is like a red, red rose	D	D-A
26. O this is no' my ain lassie	B♭	B♭-F
27. Bonny Strathyre	G	B-D
28. Over the sea to Skye	G	D-D
29. The lea-rig	D	A-D
30. A rosebud by my early walk	D	A-F♯
31. Jock o' Hazeldean	E♭	B♭-E♭
32. The Isle of Mull	B♭	D-F
33. Lord Ronald	F	C-D
34. The lass of Patie's mill	C	C-G
35. The Flowers o' the Forest	G	D-E
36. Scots, wha hae wi' Wallace bled	A	C♯-E
37. Ay waukin', O!	E	E-F♯

85

Index of First Lines

Index of Titles